Selling Skills for HR Professionals

How to Obtain Support for Ideas and New Programs

Selling Skills for HR Professionals

How to Obtain Support for Ideas and New Programs

M. Michael Markowich, DPA

American Compensation Association

American Compensation Association
14040 N. Northsight Blvd.
Scottsdale, AZ 85260
602/951-9191   Fax 602/483-8352
Fax-on-Demand 602/922-2080   http://www.acaonline.org

Editing: Andrea Healey

Contents

Preface

To succeed in their jobs, human resources professionals continuously need to convince employees to accept changes in their compensation, benefits and other HR programs. The successful professional thinks and acts tactically to convince decision makers to support recommended ideas. This involves uncovering and identifying potentially invisible players in the decision-making process and developing proposals that meet customers' needs.

The ideal approach to selling decision makers on your ideas is to have others "want to do" rather than "have to do" your proposals. As logical as this approach may sound, it can be a difficult task to achieve. Much depends on how those being affected are sold on "the doing."

Many HR professionals are uncomfortable with the idea of having to sell. Traditionally, HR professionals have relied on their knowledge of regulations to push their ideas – not necessarily their sales acumen. Consequently, they may not fully understand what it takes to be successful in selling. This lack of expertise places HR professionals at a disadvantage. While knowledge of HR core technology is important, being able to cultivate and build customer relationships is often more important. The term "customer" is used throughout this publication in reference to the various constituencies the HR professional needs to serve. Customers can include everyone from the chairman of the board to entry-level workers, as well as the actual people who purchase goods or services from the company.

The aim of this publication is to help HR professionals succeed by convincing others to accept their ideas and proposals for new programs. Strategies and tactics described are applicable to all industries, regardless of company size, profit status or whether the company's work force is unionized. Examples are based on the actual experiences of HR professionals. An HR professional may have a great idea to help the company, but it is only valuable if that proposal finds its way into customers' hands.

1
Simple vs. Complex Sales

The most common sale is a simple sale. In a simple sale, the buyer has complete power to buy, and the salesperson's objective is to close the sale in almost any way. Success is based on the salesperson's skill at one-to-one selling – traditional sales acumen. In these situations, the salesperson has one chance to sell a customer. Perhaps the opportunity arises through telephone solicitations, door-to-door selling or shopping in department stores. Simple sale approaches usually consist of high-pressure and manipulative techniques that often end up alienating customers. It is no wonder that selling has a bad connotation, and the image sticks of a salesperson as a slick, fast-talking con artist.

Conversely, complex sales yield results from a consultative approach based on earned respect and confidence. In a simple sale customers often hear "Do I have a deal for you!" In contrast, the goal of the complex sale is for the customer to say, "Your service makes sense. Thanks for taking the time to help me decide the best arrangement."

With complex sales, the objective shifts away from getting the customer to buy. Instead, it is necessary first to determine if the idea or program provides value to the customer. Success is based on mutual trust and respect, which take time to build.

Sometimes the best way to earn respect and credibility is to conclude that the recommendation may not be in the customer's best interest and the HR professional should withdraw the proposal. This possibility would be an anathema in a simple sale. However, in a complex sale, the HR professional needs to build a long-term relationship based on integrity and a partnership with the customer. The objective is not a one-shot deal.

When the focus of a sale is customer-driven, selling does not have to be painful. Instead it can be rewarding and fun, especially as customers recognize the value of the HR professional.

Another characteristic of complex sales is that approval is needed from many buyers, and one influential person or group can veto the proposal or significantly delay the decision. An HR professional typically needs buy-in from many levels:

▶ The board of directors.

▶ Top management.

► Middle management.

► Affected employees, which can include the entire work force.

This list seems to include everyone. Unfortunately, one key person can either make or break the sale. Compounding matters, the HR professional may not have direct access to a key decision maker such as a member of the board. In this case, the HR professional needs a "champion" – often the HR professional's boss – to convince the decision maker to support the proposal.

Selling Skills for the HR Professional

2

The Three-Phase
Sales Model

P rofessional sales managers invest considerable time and money to help their sales forces succeed with complex sales. Complex sales are difficult even for seasoned salespeople. It is no wonder that HR professionals have difficulty obtaining support for initiatives – they are dealing with the most demanding type of sale and are expected to be successful without having any sales training. "Strategies to Enhance Success in Complex Sales" on pages 25-28 provides some tactics that can raise the odds of success. Another important tool is the Three-Phase Sales Model. (See Figures 1, 2 and 3.)

Figure 1

Phase 1
Prospecting

Find the Itch –
Provide the Scratch

Get to Know the System

Understand company culture, customs and rituals

Obtain visas

Build personal relationships

Identify Customers and Needs

Who wants change?

Who's concerned about change?

Historic perspective

Plant seeds

Understand the Power Structure

Identify key decision makers

Identify influencers

Figure 2

Phase 2
Decision-Making Process

The End Result of
Successful Lobbying

Strategies

Involve customers (swing people)

Pilot study

Ask for sanction to fail
(not asking for yes –
but do not say no)

Final Decision

System makes buy decision and feels good about it

Figure 3

Phase 3

Postmortem

Buyer Satisfaction – Not Buyer Remorse

Fulfills expectations

Quality service after purchase

Repeat business

Referrals

Phase 1: Prospecting

"Find the itch, then provide the scratch," is an analogy that fits well when discussing the importance of prospecting, which involves locating needs and providing appropriate solutions. How the HR professional identifies itches is critical.

Historically, HR professionals have been told exactly what to do. A more proactive approach is important. By getting out of the office and interacting with other managers and employees, HR professionals can determine what is needed and, more importantly, begin developing a relationship with customers. Salespeople know the value of "relationship selling," and it is just as important for HR professionals. The following steps are key.

Step 1: Get to Know the System

An HR professional needs to understand "the why" behind company policies and practices, especially those that are branded as "crazy" by the work force. Perhaps the policy was pushed by a former CEO or even a current executive. The best "historical" information can come from senior employees in the HR professional's department.

Step 2: Identify Customers and Needs

During this phase, the HR professional should establish contact with key customers and develop a rapport to facilitate future discussions. Key customers can include:

▶ Top executives.

▶ Middle managers.

▶ "Swing" people (i.e., influential nonmanagement employees).

Building relationships starts with asking to meet customers in their offices instead of the HR professional's office. People are more relaxed in their own settings, and these visits will give the HR professional opportunities to tour different areas. The goal is to learn how the HR professional can assist the customer.

New HR professionals will find visiting customers to be a quick way to learn about the company as well as how he or she can be of value. HR professionals who are established in their positions may want to use this approach to expand services in areas underserviced by human resources. With external sales, this outreach is known as expanding one's territory by adding new clients.

Step 3: Understand the Power Structure

The HR professional needs to know how decisions are made. While the formal organizational chart is instructive, there is likely to be an informal structure that has considerable impact. The formal chart shows who reports to whom, but it does not necessarily show who can influence decision makers. Knowing those influencers can help the HR professional implement recommendations. If the HR professional can earn the respect of the influencers, the influencers could become messengers to help convince decision makers. Salespeople have used "influencers" for years – they are called "third party referrals."

While the formal organizational chart is instructive, there is likely to be an informal structure that has considerable impact.

Phase 2: Decision-Making Process

A well-known sales axiom is: Executives will support your proposal for their reasons, not yours. The meaning of this statement is that while your proposal might be good for the company, it may not go anywhere unless the decision makers accept your reasons as valid. This would seem to be obvious to anyone who ever tried to convince someone to support an idea. In practice, many HR professionals miss this point. (See Figure 4.)

Before presenting a proposal, the HR professional should complete a decision-making tree worksheet that identifies key decision-making players and their feelings about a proposal. (See Figure 5.) The worksheet identifies the following four categories:

Figure 4

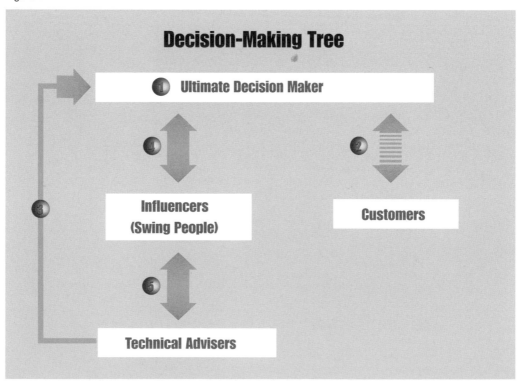

Figure 5

Decision-Making Tree Worksheet

Strategic Assessment

	S		N	O		C		
	a	b		a	b	l	m	h
1. Ultimate decision maker: Name: _____ Title: _____								
2. Customers: Name/title: _____ Name/title: _____ Name/title: _____								
3. Technical advisers: Name/title: _____ Name/title: _____ Name/title: _____ Name/title: _____								
4. Influencers: Name/title: _____ Name/title: _____ Name/title: _____ Name/title: _____								

Place an asterisk next to any technical adviser who is also an influencer.

Key:

S = Supportive
   a = believes idea is good for the company
   b = feels the idea will be personally beneficial

N = Neutral = could be for or against the idea; decision is based on what other key players do

O = Opposed
   a = believes idea is not good for the company
   b = feels the idea will not be personally beneficial

C = Credibility (of the HR professional)
   l = low
   m = moderate
   h = high

▶ **Ultimate decision maker.** These people could be the HR professional's boss, the boss's boss, the CEO, the board or a company committee. The ultimate decision maker can be identified by determining who has final authority to release the money to support the proposal, or who has final say on granting the request.

▶ **Customers affected by the recommendation.** This could include all employees, a certain group of workers, all managers, a certain group of managers, one company division and so on. Customers can be identified by determining who will personally use or supervise the use of the recommended program or policy change.

▶ **Influencers (swing people).** These are employees, either managers or nonmanagers, who are respected for their ideas and, because of their reputation, can influence how others feel. Swing people are often asked to join important task teams because company executives realize their support is important. At times, these influencers can also be technical advisers. In this case, swing people have considerable say over what gets done.

▶ **Technical advisers.** These are the employees whom the ultimate decision maker may call for technical or professional advice. They could include:

– Internal auditors.

– Payroll manager.

– Chief financial officer.

– Marketing director.

– Legal counsel.

– Computer support specialists.

- Management.

- Consultants.

Technical advisers can be identified by determining who will be asked to make judgments about the technicalities or legalities of a recommendation.

Influencers can be determined by identifying whom the decision makers listen to before making decisions. Also, determine who, by reason of position or personal relationship, can influence the boss. Sometimes, a top executive may have started employment at the same time as an entry-level worker and, because they have this in common, they may have become friends over time. The entry-level worker may have advanced to a more senior hourly position. Yet, because of the special relationship with the executive, the worker may be a source of potential support or helpful information.

After identifying each player, it should be determined whether they are supportive, neutral or opposed to the proposal. (See Figure 5.) Furthermore, identify the reason(s) for support or opposition:

▶ The idea is good/bad for the company.

▶ The idea is/is not personally beneficial to the player.

The final factor is the HR professional's perceived credibility with each player: low, moderate or high. Credibility is important because it denotes the HR professional's ability to influence others. Players who view the HR professional as highly credible will tend to accept his or her recommendations much more quickly than those who view the HR professional as having low credibility.

The HR professional may need to find other people who can influence any key players who view him or her with low credibility. This is a critical component to managing complex sales successfully. People who are neutral can be swayed based on how other key players feel, or they may be influenced by new information. The HR professional needs to develop a strategy to identify what is needed to gain a neutral person's support, just as it is important to figure out how to address or minimize opposition.

This assessment of key players and attitudes is fluid. Changes need to be made as additional information is obtained. It is important to focus on uncovering key players and determining their feelings about any proposal, especially how they feel the proposal will affect them. Politicians realize voters support candidates whom they feel will best represent their interests. HR professionals

---

The HR professional needs to develop a strategy ... to gain a neutral person's support, just as it is important to figure out how to address or minimize opposition.

---

need to realize their customers will support proposals if they believe the recommendations are in their best interests.

Phase 3: Postmortem

Just because a program is successfully implemented does not mean the project is over. Sales professionals know the importance of a program living up to the expectations it sets. Also, good programs are a salesperson's best referral for more business.

For HR professionals, successful programs are the best way to establish credibility, and credibility is money in the bank. The next time the HR professional submits a recommendation, decision makers will be more receptive in supporting it. Past success will earn the HR professional power and respect.

HR professionals need to follow up with periodic reports highlighting the impact of the new program. There is nothing better than quantitative reports – i.e., those featuring hard numbers, especially financial data or employee attitude percentages – to show value of any change. Qualitative reports, which consist of feedback from surveys and focus groups, also should be encouraged. The combination of qualitative and quantitative reports gives the HR professional an excellent one-two punch.

Marketing executives know the value of involving customers to test ideas. The same logic applies to human resources changes. It is advisable to convene a task team of customers, especially swing people, to help with the design and implementation of new HR programs. If the task team buys the new program, then others should.

Another common practice with complex changes is to phase in aspects of the program over time. This gives the company and HR professional time to assess the program's impact without risking everything at once. An alternative is to use a pilot study. The HR professional could test an idea or approach with a smaller group or with perhaps one division of a multisite company. He or she would most likely work with a group that is receptive to the change to enhance the probability of success. Now, the HR professional has a track record to obtain support to adopt the program in other areas of the company.

If the process is handled correctly, obtaining the green light to implement the program should be a logical conclusion. The process should highlight the value of the proposed change and, because key players were involved in the design and implementation, most employees will look forward to the new program.

Strategies to Enhance
Success in Complex Sales

▶ *Build personal relationships with decision makers.* Eat in the employee cafeteria. A 30-minute lunch each day equals 125 hours of annual networking. Also consider having early-morning coffee with employees at the company watering hole or participating in company social or athletic events.

▶ *Send thank you notes.* One HR manager reported receiving a thank you note from an employee whom she had thanked for serving on a company task force. The employee was touched by the HR manager's thoughtfulness.

▶ *Respond to messages in person, if possible.* Follow the example of one HR manager, who used this technique effectively to have unscheduled meetings with busy executives. And be sure to answer telephone calls and e-mail within two days. Lack of responsiveness can derail a promising career. Quick responses convey a business-like image.

▶ *Make plant rounds and visit the executive suite.* These are effective ways to make contacts. Respond quickly to comments or questions regarding HR policies. Doing something about employee concerns establishes and enhances the HR manager's image as a problem solver.

▶ *Convey the image that you're always prepared.* Get back to work quickly after vacation. And if you're new to a job, ask to work the weekend before the first day. This helps you hit the ground running.

▶ *Challenge your staff.* One new benefits director turned around negative feelings that employees had about the department's response time. The new director told company employees of her commitment to have quick and accurate responses to questions and she pledged to effect change immediately. She asked employees to call the department with any questions and, if they were not satisfied, to call her. In the interim, the new director conducted sessions with her staff to ensure they understood expectations and had the necessary information to respond accurately and quickly. The director's gambit worked, and the staff appreciated having another chance to show how good they were.

▶ *Involve the right people and share the spotlight.* If your CEO likes to speak to employees, have him or her present the new program to the work force. Actively involve swing people and anybody else in position to influence key decision makers. One HR manager spoke with an employee for about 40 minutes to resolve a benefits problem. After leaving her office, she noticed the employee spent another 30 minutes with an office assistant. The HR manager learned that the employee was seeking confirmation that the advice was correct from a trusted co-worker.

▶ *Be sensitive to customers with veto power.* Another HR manager related how a CEO's secretary delayed implementation of a companywide compensation program. All levels signed off on the proposal; however, the HR manager made a fatal political mistake. The CEO's secretary was classified at the second-highest secretarial level instead of the top – or higher – a separate category. The manager learned too late that in this company, the secretary had "veto" power.

▶ *Prepare the soil before planting seeds.* Test balloons can be useful ways to break the ice and identify a new project or idea without formally asking for approval – or even an opinion. Many professionals make the mistake of submitting proposals too quickly. It is important to assess the organization's readiness and willingness to change before proceeding with the selling process.

3

Asking the Right Questions at the Right Time

I n simple sales, questions are designed to foster a "close" in a short period of time. Salespeople often have one chance to sell the customer on a service or product, and getting a "yes" response is the key goal. Questions that force a "yes" tend to be high pressure.

In contrast, complex sales questions are designed to move players through various phases in the decision-making process. The strength of asking the right questions at the right time makes the decision to move ahead come somewhat naturally, without the HR professional having to force it. It is as if the decision to support the recommendation just evolves.

The questioning process gives the HR professional tools to navigate through the decision-making process. Getting support for ideas will no longer be a matter of luck or good timing. It is a result of a carefully planned strategic approach. Timing is essential, but timing should be considered as one aspect of a strategic plan. HR professionals do not view their own proposals as threats, but customers might. Any time an HR professional asks someone to accept a new program or policy change – even if the professional believes it is for the good – he or she is really asking that person to change.

HR professionals may not consciously think of new ideas as requiring anything negative. Nonetheless, a critical component of successful complex sales is having those who are affected accept the potential upset associated with change. Because people react differently to change, the possibility that someone will view the recommendation as threatening always exists, though the HR professional may see the proposal as extremely beneficial. That person with the negative reaction may have considerable influence over the outcome of recommendation support.

An inexperienced HR professional may underestimate this hidden factor of change, especially if the recommendation can be supported by benchmarking industry practices. Consequently, the HR professional may assume the customer or decision maker will respond in the expected manner – to support the idea. Yet, experience has shown that no matter how good the proposal or presentation may be, the information may appear unacceptable to decision makers. If this scenario is familiar, the problem is not the facts but the key player's interpretation of how the proposal affects his or her perception of the business situation.

For example, an HR professional proposed a flexible benefits program in response to the company's desire to control costs. The financial information clearly supported movement to flex, and other companies in the industry and locale had adopted a flex approach. It seemed the HR professional had done the necessary homework. However, it took this HR professional an additional three years to obtain the CEO's sanction to proceed. The reason: the CEO worried about adverse employee reaction from going flex and was more willing to support other austerity measures (e.g., wage freezes and layoffs). Finally, the CEO agreed when the costs from not going flex became greater than going flex.

The costs in this situation were not just financial but also psychological in terms of the effect on the work force. The HR professional understood the CEO's concern and waited for the right opening to revisit flex instead of discarding the idea after it was initially rejected.

With complex sales, it is necessary to clearly understand key players' perceptions and then ultimately to provide them with acceptable ways to meet their needs. This can occur by asking the right question at the right time. One case in point is Ronald Reagan's question during the 1980 presidential campaign: "Are you better off today than you were four years ago?" It made people think, and some campaign experts feel this one question clarified why voters should vote for Reagan. Questions have power. The key is knowing what to say and when to say it.

If asked correctly, questions can enhance the probability of sales success without alienating other people. Even if the eventual conclusion is "no," an HR professional does not want to burn bridges because a "no" today may become a "yes" tomorrow. The "Question Cycle" identifies the sequence of questions that eventually lead to obtaining desired support. (See Figure 6.) Following are the major types of questions.

Phase 1: Ice Breaker Questions

These nonthreatening questions are used to begin a discussion. Examples include asking about:

▶ The number of employees covered by a plan.

▶ Current benefit costs.

▶ History of employee reactions upon changing benefit designs.

▶ Top management's views on involving employees in change programs.

While asking these questions, the HR professional must not go overboard. Too many ice breaker questions can bore or anger the person being questioned.

Phase 2: Fishing Questions

These probing questions are asked to uncover potential problems, difficulties and dissatisfactions in areas where the HR professional can help. Answers give guidance to perceived needs and possible solutions. Some examples:

▶ Why is it that nonhighly compensated employees do not contribute enough to the 401(k) plan? What do you believe could be done to motivate nonhighly compensated employees to contribute more?

▶ What is your current absentee control program? How effective do you believe it is?

▶ What is the current pay system? Why does the company want to move to a

Figure 6

The Question Cycle –
Asking the Right Questions at the Right Time

Phase ① The HR professional uses

ICE BREAKER QUESTIONS ...

Phase ② To set the stage for

FISHING QUESTIONS ...

To find out from the client/customer

PROBLEMS, NEEDS, DIFFICULTIES ...

Phase ③ Which are clarified

BY ASKING FULL DISCLOSURE QUESTIONS ...

Which help customers understand the seriousness
of an issue and identify possible solutions

Phase ④ And leads to

VISUAL BENEFIT QUESTIONS ...

Whereby the buyer states value/benefit of proposal

Phase ⑤ **HR PROFESSIONAL ASKS CLOSING QUESTIONS ...**

And

ACHIEVES DESIRED SUPPORT

pay for performance approach? Who is promoting the change? Has the company ever attempted a pay for performance program? If yes, what happened? If no, why not?

Phase 3: Full Disclosure Questions

These questions take the customer's initial problem and explore the full effects and consequences. Full disclosure questions give customers a clearer understanding of the seriousness of the problem and identify possible solutions. Some examples:

▶ What is the effect of reducing the unscheduled absence rate by 10 percent or $500,000 per year?

▶ If employees understood investment strategies, would they increase their 401(k) contributions?

▶ Would management be willing to involve employees in designing a program that would give workers extra money if bottom-line objectives were met?

Phase 4: Visual Benefit Questions

The stage is set for the HR professional to obtain tangible support for an action plan addressing the customer's acknowledged need. Of particular importance is for the customer to verbalize the benefits of adopting a proposal. The HR professional wants the customer to believe the idea or proposal has value. The best way to know is for the customer to actually say so. Examples of visual benefit questions are:

▶ How does the proposal appear to meet your needs?

▶ If a task force of employees likes the approach to financial education, would you be willing to have it presented on company time?

▶ If the CFO felt the absentee control program would save the company money, could we progress with a group of employees to work out the details?

▶ If we could structure a pay for performance approach that would not be an "entitlement" program, would top management buy it?

▶ Would you be willing to work with management to develop a team incentive program in which employees would receive extra money for meeting bottom-line objectives?

The answer should lead the HR professional and customers to the final stage – the close.

Phase 5: The Close

A salesperson's ultimate goal is to close. However, in complex sales, the decision to accept the HR professional's recommendation seems to evolve naturally – it just makes sense to the customer. It is not a hard decision, but one the customer believes will address a pressing issue.

4

Two Case Studies

The following two case studies are based on real-life situations. They illustrate exactly how the complex sales process works and demonstrate techniques that can help HR professionals succeed in selling their programs.

Case Study 1: A No-Fault Absentee Program

A new HR manager began the sales process by asking managers and employees for their views of how the HR program could be enhanced to address their needs. This prospecting gave the HR manager a jump-start in getting to know the system and building relationships with key players. From the discussions, the HR manager uncovered a perceived need to have an effective attendance policy.

Managers complained that although the current attendance policy rewarded excellent attendance, it was ineffective against abusers. Employees complained that the current system penalized good employees with good attendance because abusers seemed to take time off whenever they wanted while employees with good attendance ended up doing more work. This historical perspective enabled the HR manager to better understand what managers and employees were looking for and why.

The HR manager had succeeded with an approach she had tried at a previous employer called No-Fault. The approach is an objective and equitable way to manage excessive absenteeism. Although many organizations and surveys have reported No-Fault to be effective and supported by employees, the concept is not without controversy and takes time to implement.

This historical perspective enabled the HR manager to better understand what managers and employees were looking for and why.

To break the ice, the HR manager decided to float a test balloon at the company's Human Resource Committee Meeting (an advisory group composed of a cross-section of managers) by describing how No-Fault worked.

As often occurs with new ideas, members had mixed feelings. Some felt the No-Fault concept was "too off the wall" for top management and employees to accept. Others liked it. The HR manager asked members to think about the concept for further discussion at the next quarterly meeting. During the interim, the HR manager encouraged committee members to talk to their supervisors and employees about the pros and cons of No-Fault. The HR manager left the meeting encouraged. The discussion was the first step in getting No-Fault eventually implemented. Because No-Fault was somewhat controversial, the HR manager had expected some resistance. However, issues were on the table and, most important, a seed had been planted.

Between meetings, the HR manager reviewed the No-Fault approach with line executives and other pivotal managers (e.g., the payroll and data-processing managers). The HR manager knew it was important to personally find out who favored No-Fault and who had reservations. Knowing how executives felt helped her understand the power structure and strategize the best way to eventually sell No-Fault.

At the next committee meeting, members still had mixed feelings. However, the HR manager sensed some support, so an option was raised. The HR manager proposed that a No-Fault approach be pilot tested with a group of managers and employees who liked the concept. In this way, those who had reservations could wait for the outcomes, and those who favored it could try the approach. The committee agreed to the recommendation, and this support was invaluable for obtaining top management's endorsement to move ahead with the pilot approach.

The next step was to convene a task force of swing people to work with the HR manager and members of the committee to develop the No-Fault policy. The task force took six months to develop a policy, and the pilot lasted nine months. The task force and the committee jointly reviewed the results. The decision was to implement the No-Fault approach companywide.

In reality, the HR manager was the facilitator of change. She was not seen as "selling" a program, though, in retrospect, the best salespeople are rarely seen as salespeople. They are viewed as problem solvers and agents of change. Isn't this what HR managers are expected to be?

Case Study 2: An Alternative Reward Program

The literature highlights the growth of alternative reward programs such as gainsharing, profit sharing, stock options and bonuses. The hope is that employees will be motivated to find ways to enhance operations, especially if they can share in the "spoils."

However, these programs are not without risk, both to the company and employees. Of particular concern is employee buy-in to the notion that additional compensation is not an entitlement but rather is based on bottom-line results. This means employees must be willing to invest extra effort with no guarantee of extra money – not an easy sell.

Two executives of a community hospital of 800 employees used a nontraditional way to launch the development of a gainsharing program. The HR manager, with the hospital's nursing executive, presented a radical reward possibility to a group of nursing personnel (about 185 RNs, LPNs, nurse assistants and unit clerks). The idea was to develop a program to enhance the quality of patient care. The reward for achievement of excellence was extra money. The ground rules were clear:

▶ **Rule 1**: Patient care improvements had to be supported by objective documentation.

▶ **Rule 2**: This was to be a team effort because the team takes care of patients more so than any one person. (A side benefit was to enhance team effectiveness.)

▶ **Rule 3**: Reward money had to come from documented savings. The CFO had to sign off before any extra money was distributed.

As expected, the group had many questions. However, the executives were selling an idea, not a developed program. Also, (this is the radical part) the employees were given the right to refuse to participate in the program. In essence, employees had the veto power. They could say, "We're not interested," and the idea would die on the table without any hard feelings. The two executives felt success was based on employee willingness to work with management to see if they could develop something new. Clarity in expectations resulted from stating the ground rules up front and by giving the staff the "right of first refusal."

As it turned out, the specialty care units (emergency unit, cardiac care, intensive care) declined to participate. However, the medical/surgical units agreed.

It took about 10 months to develop the program. One year from the initial meetings, the program was launched and was successful.

This was not a "hard sell" because the staff was not pressured into working with management. In contrast, in a simple but powerful way, it demonstrated an approach to foster buy-in by giving employees the right to say "no."

Success with alternative reward programs is significantly influenced by employees' willingness to play by new rules. Clearly, there are many steps to build a successful alternative reward program. Two crucial conditions are:

▶ Employee acceptance that the program is not an entitlement.

▶ Employee willingness to work with management to develop program components, especially objective evaluation criteria.

5

Closing the Deal

A 1995 study of HR competencies conducted by the Society for Human Resource Management (SHRM) and Commerce Clearing House (CCH) highlighted the perception that knowledgeable HR professionals typically do not get as much visibility and credit as their counterparts in finance and line management. The study's respondents said the key to raising credibility is enhancing communication skills and the ability to consult with and influence others. These competencies are integral parts of the selling process.

HR executives who feel
comfortable with selling see
visibility as an important step
in building credibility.

Obtaining support for ideas is another way of consulting with and influencing the boss and other key people. When they assume a sales role, HR professionals find themselves playing the role of a messenger. HR executives who feel comfortable with selling see visibility as an important step in building credibility. And it is credibility that gives HR professionals the power to influence others while achieving personal visibility.

The sales cycle or ritual is composed of a series of plateaus. It is rare that an initial discussion results in the acceptance of a new idea. It is similar to a person walking into a car dealership and paying the sticker price without trying to negotiate a lower price. Closing a complex sale often takes longer than expected, and unexpected obstacles are the norm. However, a key ingredient for success is knowing what to ask and when. If nothing else, good questions will save the HR professional time, effort and perhaps money. It is also important to be patient because complex sales take time. It is not unusual for an HR professional to invest two to three years before convincing a company to implement a new program.

Alvin and Heidi Tofflers' book *Creating a New Civilization* outlines a blueprint for success in the information era. The authors argue that success in the information era requires a different way of thinking and behaving. Everyone from entry-level workers to the CEO will be affected. A key strategic question for businesses is how to use human resources programs as motivators to achieve profitability objectives. Solutions will require a change in habits and probably will challenge longstanding beliefs and values. Therefore, resistance is to be expected.

So, how can HR professionals obtain support for their ideas in this climate? It is hoped that techniques and tactics described in this booklet will provide some guidance. We know that success in today's ever-changing environment requires new ways of thinking. The radical thought for HR professionals is to view sales acumen as an essential skill for success as a leader of business change.

 **M. Michael Markowich, DPA,** is a nationally known human resources consultant, author and speaker specializing in the design and implementation of paid time off banks and no-fault absentee approaches. His clients are from a cross-section of industries ranging in size from 65 to 11,000 employees, profit and nonprofit, union and nonunion. Other services include educational programs on retirement planning, effective disciplinary action and conflict resolution, and organizational/management development. His background includes training and management positions within union and nonunion companies, including 10 years as Vice President of Human Resources for a multifacility corporation. He has published five national award-winning articles and has authored more than 100 articles on a variety of HR and management topics. Markowich is a frequent speaker at national conferences, and he is on the faculty of ACA and the Temple University School of Business. He is a member of the Commerce Clearing House Board of Advisors on HR Management and conducts CCH's annual survey on unscheduled absences. He presents professional development programs for Cornell, Rutgers and Michigan State universities. Markowich holds an M.B.A in organizational development from Drexel University and a doctorate in public administration from Nova University. He is based in Huntingdon Valley, Pa.

ACA welcomes comments regarding this publication
and topic ideas for future publications.
Please contact ACA Publications at the address below.

Global Remuneration
Organisation

American Compensation Association
14040 N. Northsight Blvd., Scottsdale, AZ 85260
Telephone 602/951-9191   Fax 602/483-8352
E-mail *bblocks@acaonline.org*